RATTLESNAKES

Published by Creative Education, Inc., 123 South Broad Street, Mankato, Minnesota
56001

Library of Congress Cataloging-in-Publication Data

Hurst, Beth Wagner.
Rattlesnakes / by Beth Wagner Hurst and Bob Dorn.
p.   cm. — (Zoobooks)
Summary: Describes the physical characteristics and behavior of the rattlesnake and
presents rattlesnake-related activities.
ISBN 0-88682-426-5
1. Rattlesnakes—Juvenile literature. [1. Rattlesnakes. 2. Snakes.] I. Dorn, Bob. II.
Title. III. Series: Zoo books (Mankato, Minn.)
QL666.O69H87   1991   599.96—dc20   91-11776 CIP AC

RATTLESNAKES

Series Created by
John Bonnett Wexo

Written by
Beth Wagner Brust
Bob Dorn

Zoological Consultant
Charles R. Schroeder, D.V.M.
Director Emeritus
San Diego Zoo &
San Diego Wild Animal Park

Scientific Consultant
Charles Radcliffe, Ph.D.
Department of Herpetology
Zoological Society of San Diego

Creative Education

Art Credits

Main Art: Tim Hayward. **Page Eight, Left:** Walter Stuart; **Pages Eight and Nine, Bottom:** Nick Corleoné; **Page Four, Center:** Walter Stuart; **Page Twelve, Center Left and Right:** Walter Stuart; **Lower Left,** Walter Stuart; **Pages Twelve and Thirteen, Upper Center:** Nick Corleoné; **Page Thirteen, Upper Right:** Nancy Isbell; **Lower Left,** Nancy Isbell; **Pages Twenty and Twenty-one, Lower Center:** Walter Stuart; **Page Twenty-one, Upper Right:** Fiona King; **Lower Right,** Walter Stuart; **Activities Art** by Darrel Millsap.

Our Thanks To: Kent G. Osborne (San Diego Zoo), Bernard Thornton, Susan Lacy, Paul Brust, Sean Brust, Joe Selig.

Photographic Credits

Cover: Zoological Society of San Diego; **Pages Six and Seven:** Robert T. Zappalorti (Nature's Images); **Page Nine:** David Kronen (Herp-Osteo); **Page Ten, Lower Left:** Veronica Tagland (Wildlife Education, Ltd.); **Pages Ten and Eleven, Upper Center:** Steve Kaufman (Bruce Coleman, Ltd.); **Page Eleven, Left:** Leonard Lee Rue III (Bruce Coleman, Ltd.); **Right:** Peter B. Kaplan (Photo Researchers); **Page Twelve:** Ken Kelley (Zoological Society of San Diego); **Page Thirteen:** Fred Whitehead (Animals Animals); **Page Fourteen:** Veronica Tagland (Wildlife Education, Ltd.); **Page Fifteen:** K.G. Vock/Okapia (Photo Researchers); **Page Sixteen: Upper Right,** Veronica Tagland (Wildlife Education, Ltd.); **Center,** Alan Blank (Bruce Coleman, Inc.); **Lower Left, Center, and Right:** Walker Van Riper (University of Colorado, Boulder); **Page Seventeen:** Veronica Tagland (Wildlife Education, Ltd.); **Page Eighteen:** Jane Burton (Bruce Coleman, Ltd.); **Page Nineteen, Lower Right:** Tom McHugh (Photo Researchers); **Inside Back Cover, All Photos:** Rodney Jones San Diego.

Contents

Rattlesnakes have a bad reputation. Many people think of them as dangerous snakes that can kill a person with a single bite from their poisonous fangs. For this reason, they are feared—and perhaps even hated.

There is no doubt that rattlesnakes *can* be dangerous to people. In fact, that is one reason why you should read this book—to find out more about the danger, and to learn *how to avoid* it. But more than that, you will find out that rattlesnakes are *one of the most fascinating groups of animals on earth.*

For example, the same things that make rattlesnakes dangerous also make them *wonderful hunters.* Their poisonous fangs are probably the most amazing hunting tools found in nature. And rattlesnakes have special ways of finding their prey that will astonish you—including a "high tech" system that they can use to locate animals *in total darkness*!

You will also discover that rattlers are actually *beautiful* animals, when you look closely at them (from a safe distance, of course). There are more than 30 different kinds, and most of them are decorated with truly elegant patterns and colors.

Rattlesnakes get their name from *the rattles* on their tails. They are the *only* snakes that have them. If you look at the rattle on the snake at right, you will see that it is made up of *sections.* Every year, up to three new sections may be added, until some rattles get very large—with *20 or more sections.*

The sound of the rattle can be very loud, and the noise can carry for long distances—up to 60 feet (18 meters). The main purpose of the rattle may surprise you. It is used to *warn* people and large animals *to stay away.* It seems that rattlesnakes don't want to run into you any more than you want to run into them!

The more you find out about rattlesnakes, the more you will see that they are not evil animals at all. Like lions and tigers, they hunt to survive. It may be hard for people to love rattlesnakes, but we should certainly *appreciate them* for the wonderful creatures they are.

The body of a rattlesnake is long and rather narrow. Like other snakes, rattlers hunt small animals for food. Usually, they wait alongside trails and catch their prey by surprising it. But sometimes they need to follow the animals into their holes to catch them. Their long, narrow bodies make it easier for them to do this.

At the front end of the body, there is a rather large head, with large eyes and a dangerous mouth. At the back, there is a tail with a rattle on it. Rattlesnakes are the *only* snakes with rattles on their tails.

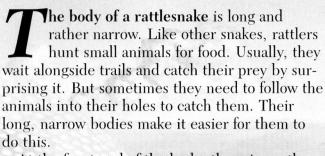

Rattlesnakes are divided into two groups. Most are part of the *Crotalus* (Crow-TAL-luss) group, which includes the larger rattlers with broad heads. The snakes in the other group, called *Sistrurus* (Siss-TRUE-rus), are smaller, with narrower heads. They have *9 large scales* on their heads.

SISTRURUS   CROTALUS

The long and narrow shape of the body mea that everything *inside the body* must be long and narrow, too. As yo can see, a rattlesnake' stomach Ⓐ is very lon And so is everything else!

Some people think that rattlesnakes are almost all tail. But the tail is really only a small part. The body (*shown in blue*) is much bigger.

Rattlesnake bodies are wider in the middle than the bodies of most other snakes. This allows them to eat larger prey. And they have large stomachs to hold the prey they catch.

HEAD   BODY

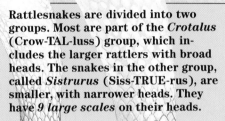

A rattlesnake has only one lung Ⓑ—but *what a lung!* It stretches almost 3/4 of the total body length. If you had a lung like that, it would stretch from your neck down to your knees!

The rattle at the end of the tail is used to give warnings to other animals and to humans. When a rattlesnake shakes its rattle, it is saying *"Go away or I may bite you!"* It can shake the rattle very fast—up to *50 times a second.* The sound it makes is a loud buzz.

me rattlesnakes grow to be ry long—more than *6 feet long* .8 meters). And they may weigh much as 15 pounds (6.8 kilo- ams). But most of them are aller than that.

TAIL

Rattlesnakes have wonderful skeletons, with *hundreds* of bones in them. A long back- bone runs down the center of the back Ⓒ, and there are many curved ribs at- tached to it. The skeleton is both *strong and flexible.* The snake can easily bend it into a round coil.

The skin of a rattlesnake is very important in the life of the snake. Down on the ground, there are plenty of rocks and thorns and other things that can scrape and cut the body of a rattler. So its skin has to be *tough on the outside* to protect the body. At the same time, the skin has to be *flexible enough* to allow the snake to move freely.

Rattlesnakes have *three layers* of skin. The bottom layer is the thickest, and has the true color of the skin. The middle layer is thick and tough for protection. And there is *an extra layer* on top for extra protection. From time to time, the top layer peels off.

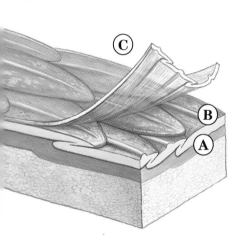

The middle layer of skin is folded in many places to make it thicker. The thickest parts are called *the scales* Ⓐ of the rattler. There are thousands of scales, and they form a coat of armor that protects the body very well. The scales *overlap*, so they can slide back and forth a little and allow the snake to move.

As the snake slithers along on the ground, the outer layer of skin Ⓑ gets scratched and cut by rocks and other hard objects. About twice a year, the outer layer *peels off* Ⓒ.

A rattlesnake *keeps growing* as long as it lives. And this is another reason why it must shed its outer layer of skin again and again. As it grows, it needs *a larger skin*—just as you need larger clothes when you get too big for your old clothes.

To shed the outer layer of skin, a rattlesnake starts rubbing its head against something hard. The skin begins to peel away, and the snake can wiggle out of it.

As the outer layer of skin comes off, it turns *inside out*. Underneath the old outer layer, a new and shiny outer layer has already grown. This makes the rattler look like a new snake.

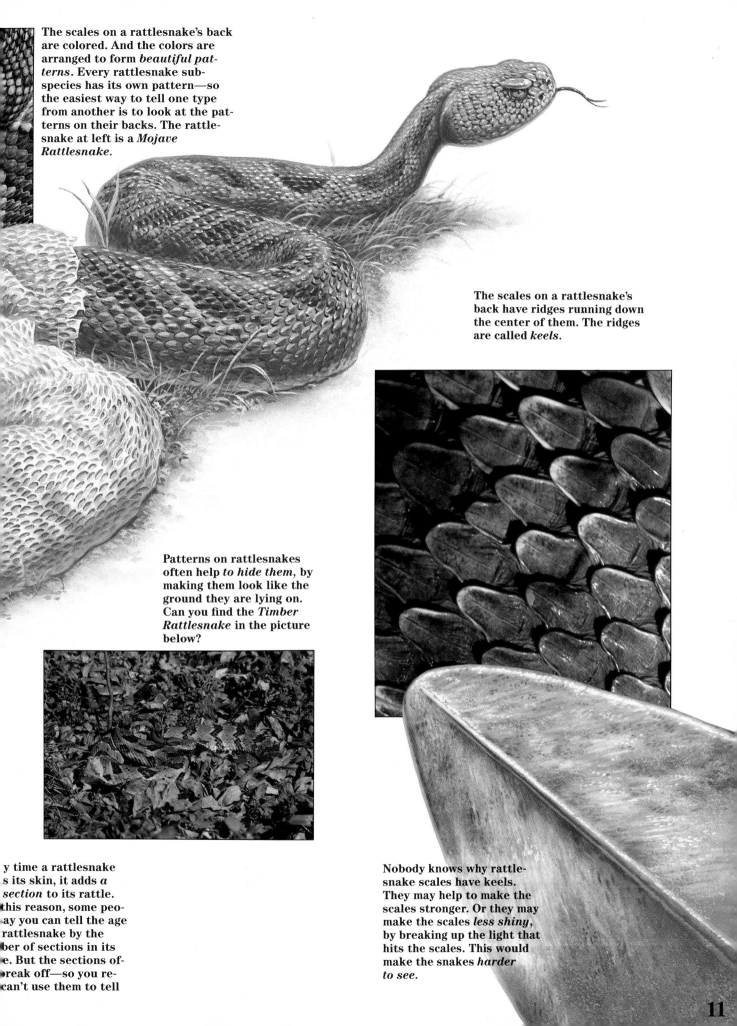

The scales on a rattlesnake's back are colored. And the colors are arranged to form *beautiful patterns*. Every rattlesnake subspecies has its own pattern—so the easiest way to tell one type from another is to look at the patterns on their backs. The rattlesnake at left is a *Mojave Rattlesnake*.

The scales on a rattlesnake's back have ridges running down the center of them. The ridges are called *keels*.

Patterns on rattlesnakes often help *to hide them*, by making them look like the ground they are lying on. Can you find the *Timber Rattlesnake* in the picture below?

y time a rattlesnake
s its skin, it adds *a
section* to its rattle.
this reason, some peo-
ay you can tell the age
rattlesnake by the
ber of sections in its
e. But the sections of-
reak off—so you re-
can't use them to tell

Nobody knows why rattlesnake scales have keels. They may help to make the scales stronger. Or they may make the scales *less shiny*, by breaking up the light that hits the scales. This would make the snakes *harder to see*.

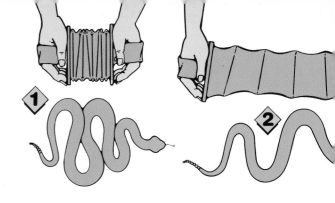

Moving around without legs may look hard, but rattlesnakes are very good at it. In fact, they have *four different ways* of moving on the ground. If one way doesn't get them very far, they'll try another. Sometimes, on very smooth surfaces, they have to try all four.

When a rattlesnake moves, its strong muscles ripple its scales from head to tail. The ripples are short movements that propel the snake forward. Each motion is so tiny that the snake seems to slide along with no effort.

One way a rattlesnake moves is called *Concertina motion*—because the snake moves its body like an old-fashioned accordion, or concertina (con-sur-TEEN-uh). First, the snake bunches up its body (1). Next, it holds the back part of its tail in place and pushes the front part of its body forward (2). Finally, the snake pulls the back part of its body forward (3).

As each scute digs in, muscles pull it back toward the tail (C). One by one, the scutes push against the ground— and this moves the snake forward.

Caterpillar motion can move a snake in a straight line. So rattlesnakes use this kind of motion in tight places. To push its body forward, a snake moves *the large scutes* on the bottom of the body (A). One after another, the scutes dig into the ground like small shovels (B).

Here is wh▶ scutes loo◀ close up.

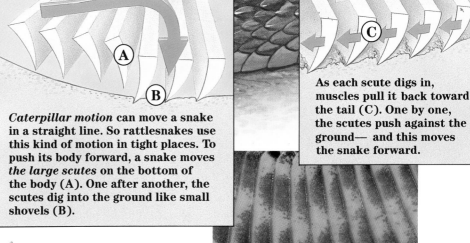

When a snake moves in a straight line, it uses the same technique that people use when they row a boat. It digs its scutes into the ground the way rowers dig their oars into the water. The rest of the body is then pulled along, just the way a boat is pulled forward in the water.

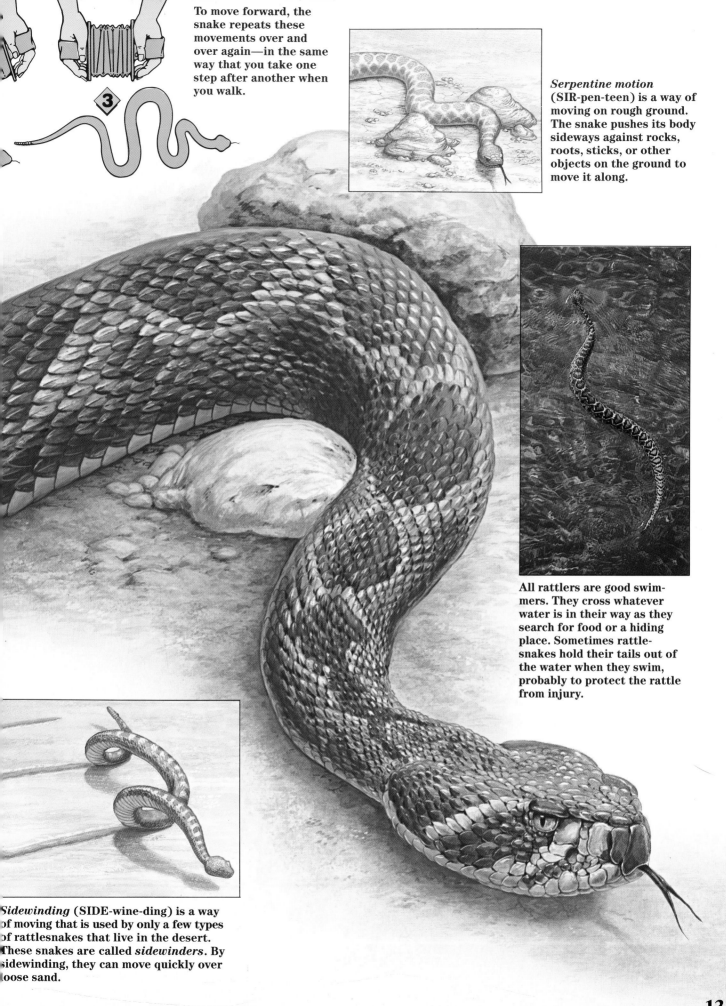

To move forward, the snake repeats these movements over and over again—in the same way that you take one step after another when you walk.

Serpentine motion (SIR-pen-teen) is a way of moving on rough ground. The snake pushes its body sideways against rocks, roots, sticks, or other objects on the ground to move it along.

All rattlers are good swimmers. They cross whatever water is in their way as they search for food or a hiding place. Sometimes rattlesnakes hold their tails out of the water when they swim, probably to protect the rattle from injury.

Sidewinding (SIDE-wine-ding) is a way of moving that is used by only a few types of rattlesnakes that live in the desert. These snakes are called *sidewinders*. By sidewinding, they can move quickly over loose sand.

Rattlesnakes have wonderful senses that help them to hunt. Using their senses, they can find prey at any time of the day or night. They can even locate warm-blooded animals *in complete darkness*!

When we humans want to find something, we use our eyes and ears the most. Rattlesnakes have eyes and ears, and they sometimes use them to find prey. But they mostly use their *sense of smell* and their *sense of heat* to hunt.

All rattlesnakes are *pit vipers* (VY-purrs). This means that they have special openings called *pits* on their faces that *can feel heat*. Even in complete darkness, the pits can "see" the heat that is given off by the bodies of warm-blooded animals. The animals can try to hide, by staying still and quiet—but the heat from their bodies gives them away.

SENSE OF SMELL AND HEAT

SENSE OF SIGHT

SENSE OF H

Different senses are used to find prey at different distances. When animals are far away, the snake can "hear" faint vibrations of the ground that are caused by their feet. Closer up, the rattler can see the animals. At the closest distances, the snake can use its tongue or its pits.

The ears of a rattlesnake are *inside the head*. There are no ear openings on the outside.

To hear, rattlesnakes use *their jawbones*! They rest their jaws on the ground to pick up vibrations that are made by animals (or people) that are moving nearby. The jawbone carries the vibrations to the ear inside the head.

S
T

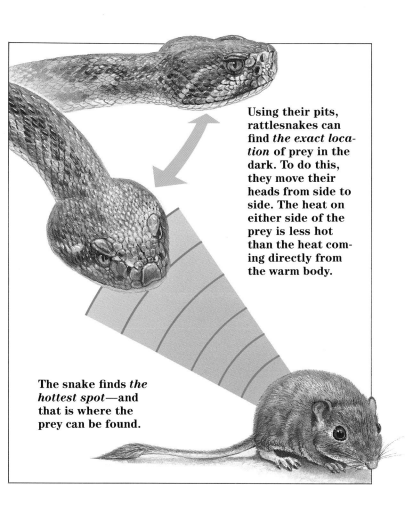

Using their pits, rattlesnakes can find *the exact location* of prey in the dark. To do this, they move their heads from side to side. The heat on either side of the prey is less hot than the heat coming directly from the warm body.

The snake finds *the hottest spot*—and that is where the prey can be found.

Rattlesnakes can see well only at *short distances*—up to 15 feet (4.6 meters). All rattlesnakes have large eyes with pupils that can be opened very wide, to help them see in very dim light. There are *no eyelids* on the eyes—so when rattlesnakes sleep, their eyes stay open!

The bodies of warm-blooded animals give off heat.

The pits on a rattlesnake's face can feel the heat.

To smell, a rattlesnake uses *its tongue*. The moist tongue is flicked out to pick up smells from the air and ground. Then the tongue carries the smells *into the mouth*, where they are "tasted" by a special sense organ called Jacobson's organ. A rattler can also use its nostrils for smelling.

HING
SCENT

T he poison of rattlesnakes is used to catch prey, and to protect the snakes. Some people think that rattlesnakes go around biting everything in sight, just to be "mean." But this is not true. They only use their poison to catch their food—or when they feel they are in danger.

Rattlesnake poison is called *venom* (VEN-um). The venom is made in special glands inside a rattler's head, and it is injected into prey through hollow *fangs*. The snakes can control the amount of venom that they put into prey. They usually inject *just enough venom* to kill the prey quickly.

The fangs of rattlesnakes are *hollow*, like the needles that doctors use to give injections. They have sharp, pointed ends that can break through skin.

Ⓔ

A rattlesnake can strike prey that is very close to its head from almost any position. But to strike an animal that is more than a few inches away, it throws the front half of its body forward, then sinks its fangs into the prey.

Venom is pushed through the hollow fangs and into the prey. *The amount* of venom that is injected depends on *the size* of the prey. In general, a rattlesnake will use less venom for smaller prey and more venom for larger prey.

Ⓐ Ⓑ

The fangs of a rattlesnake are usually folded inside the mouth Ⓐ. They move forward Ⓑ when the snake strikes.

The strike has three stages. First, the body lunges forward with the jaws only half open. The fangs are still folded up inside the mouth.

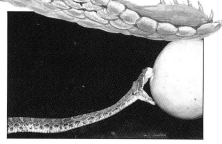

Just before the mouth reaches the prey, the fangs swing down. They break through the skin and begin to sink into the body of the prey.

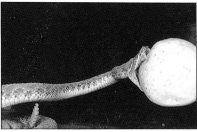

As the fangs sink deeper, the snake begins to inject the venom. The deeper the venom is injected, the better chance it will have to kill the prey.

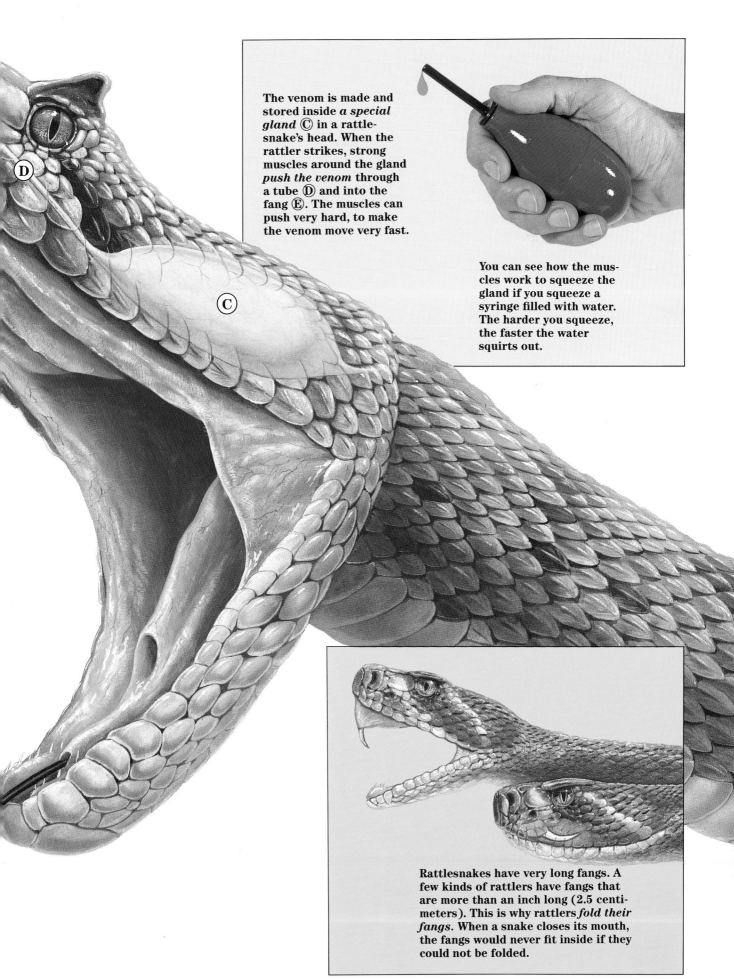

The venom is made and stored inside *a special gland* Ⓒ in a rattlesnake's head. When the rattler strikes, strong muscles around the gland *push the venom* through a tube Ⓓ and into the fang Ⓔ. The muscles can push very hard, to make the venom move very fast.

You can see how the muscles work to squeeze the gland if you squeeze a syringe filled with water. The harder you squeeze, the faster the water squirts out.

Rattlesnakes have very long fangs. A few kinds of rattlers have fangs that are more than an inch long (2.5 centimeters). This is why rattlers *fold their fangs*. When a snake closes its mouth, the fangs would never fit inside if they could not be folded.

When a rattlesnake hunts, it takes its time. It doesn't rush around chasing prey. Instead, it moves slowly and carefully—or it may simply *wait in one spot* for prey to come along.

When it strikes, it can move incredibly fast. But then, it usually doesn't try to eat the prey right away. It sits back and waits for the venom to kill the prey— and then it slowly swallows the food without any fuss.

Rattlesnakes often hunt at night, when their ability to "see" in the dark with their heat-sensing pits gives them *a special advantage.* But they may hunt at any time of the day or night. Their favorite prey are rodents, like mice, rats, and gophers. But they also feed on birds, lizards, frogs, and toads.

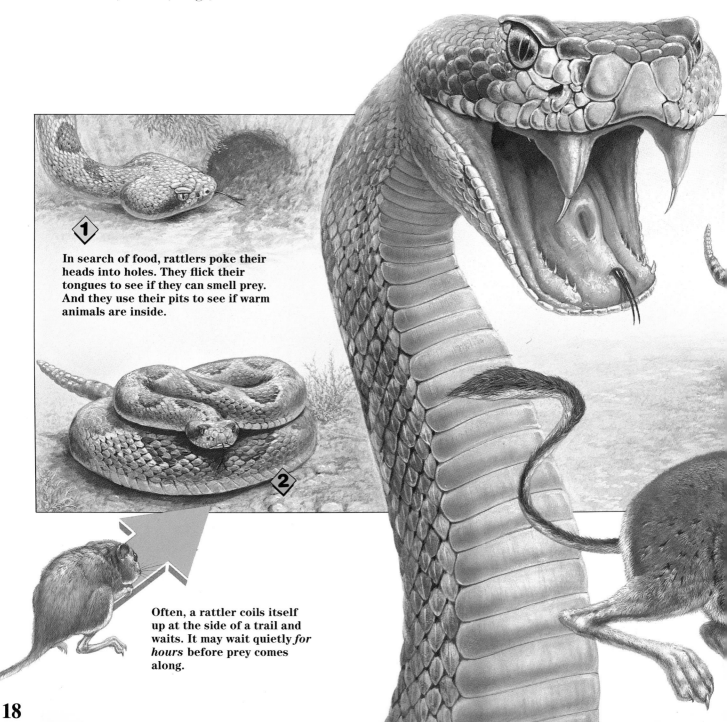

1

In search of food, rattlers poke their heads into holes. They flick their tongues to see if they can smell prey. And they use their pits to see if warm animals are inside.

2

Often, a rattler coils itself up at the side of a trail and waits. It may wait quietly *for hours* before prey comes along.

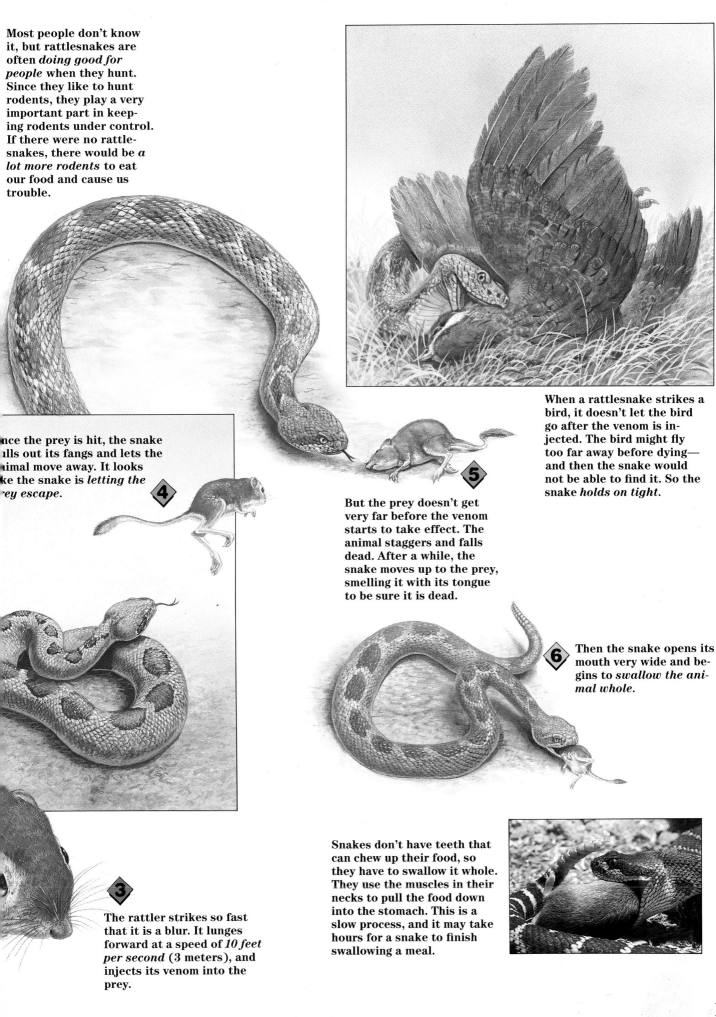

Most people don't know it, but rattlesnakes are often *doing good for people* when they hunt. Since they like to hunt rodents, they play a very important part in keeping rodents under control. If there were no rattlesnakes, there would be *a lot more rodents* to eat our food and cause us trouble.

When a rattlesnake strikes a bird, it doesn't let the bird go after the venom is injected. The bird might fly too far away before dying—and then the snake would not be able to find it. So the snake *holds on tight*.

Once the prey is hit, the snake pulls out its fangs and lets the animal move away. It looks like the snake is *letting the prey escape*.

4

5

But the prey doesn't get very far before the venom starts to take effect. The animal staggers and falls dead. After a while, the snake moves up to the prey, smelling it with its tongue to be sure it is dead.

6

Then the snake opens its mouth very wide and begins to *swallow the animal whole*.

3

The rattler strikes so fast that it is a blur. It lunges forward at a speed of *10 feet per second* (3 meters), and injects its venom into the prey.

Snakes don't have teeth that can chew up their food, so they have to swallow it whole. They use the muscles in their necks to pull the food down into the stomach. This is a slow process, and it may take hours for a snake to finish swallowing a meal.

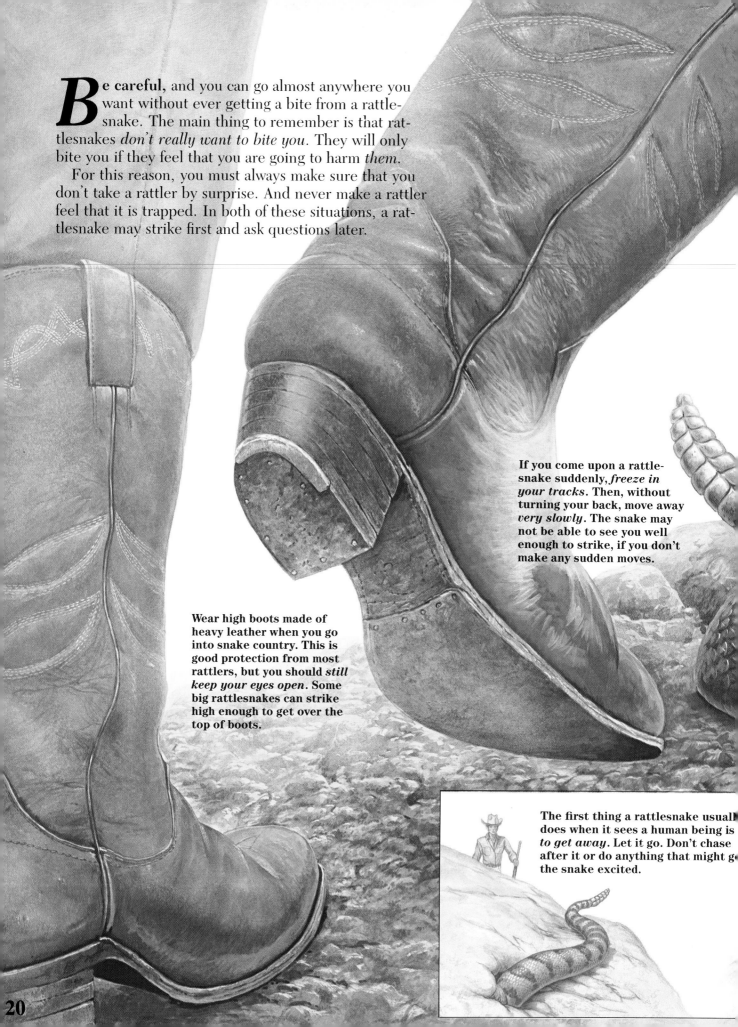

*B*e careful, and you can go almost anywhere you want without ever getting a bite from a rattlesnake. The main thing to remember is that rattlesnakes *don't really want to bite you.* They will only bite you if they feel that you are going to harm *them.*

For this reason, you must always make sure that you don't take a rattler by surprise. And never make a rattler feel that it is trapped. In both of these situations, a rattlesnake may strike first and ask questions later.

If you come upon a rattlesnake suddenly, *freeze in your tracks.* **Then, without turning your back, move away** *very slowly.* **The snake may not be able to see you well enough to strike, if you don't make any sudden moves.**

Wear high boots made of heavy leather when you go into snake country. This is good protection from most rattlers, but you should *still keep your eyes open.* **Some big rattlesnakes can strike high enough to get over the top of boots.**

The first thing a rattlesnake usuall**y does when it sees a human being is** *to get away.* **Let it go. Don't chase after it or do anything that might g**e**t the snake excited.**

Rattler Rules

To make sure that you don't surprise and anger a rattlesnake, be sure to follow these simple rules.

- *Always* look where you are putting your feet and your hands.
- *Never* reach into holes or dark places where a rattler may be hiding.
- *Always* try to stay out of tall grass, if you can—and be careful if you have to walk through it.
- *Always* gather firewood during the daytime—rattlesnakes are more active at night.
- *Always* wear thick shoes in snake country—or better yet, high boots of heavy leather.
- *Never* pick up a snake, even if it looks dead. It might not be dead, but just pretending to be.
- *Never* make quick moves if you see a rattlesnake or hear its rattle. Back up slowly—but be sure you don't back into another snake.

- *Always* try to learn what snakes live in the area you are visiting, and what they look like. This will help you to know which snakes are dangerous, and which are not.

If you are bitten by a rattlesnake:
- *Don't panic!* Remember what the snake looked like. And check to be sure that the fangs actually broke your skin.
- *Get a doctor* as soon as you can. But send somebody else to do it, if possible. If you run, your blood will pump faster and the poison will spread faster.
- *Never* try to treat a snakebite yourself, unless there is no chance of getting a doctor.

NORTH AMERICA

SOUTH AMERICA

There are rattlesnakes in almost every part of the United States. Mexico is known as "the land of rattlesnakes," because there are so many kinds there. Fewer rattlesnakes live in Central and South America—but some of them are very poisonous.

☐ *Areas where rattlesnakes are found*

In general, a rattlesnake can strike out for *half* of its body length. For example, a 6-foot rattler (2 meters) can strike to 3 feet away (1 meter). However, a rattlesnake that is *up on a ledge* may be able to strike farther.

Whatever you do, *don't try to kill the snake*. When people try to kill rattlesnakes, they often get bitten!

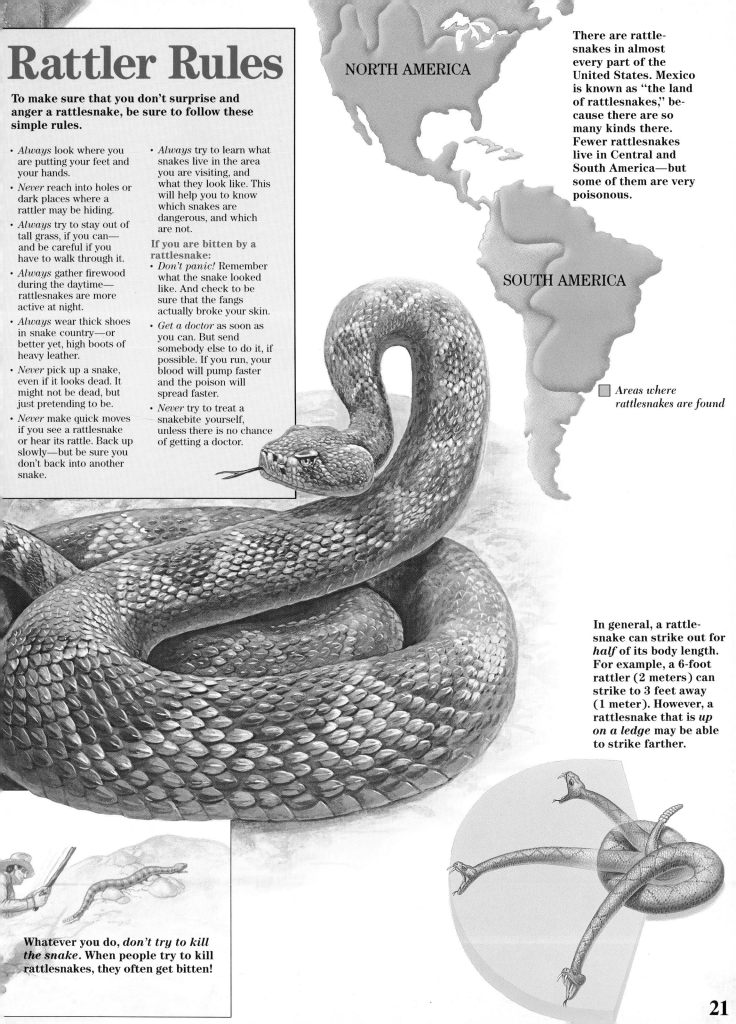

21

Rattlesnakes

FUN!

*R*attle your brain with these fun snake activities. Use what you know about rattlesnakes to solve the puzzles on these pages.

Snakey Poems

The poems above are made up of words about snakes. The words make pictures that tell even more about snakes. After enjoying these poems, try to make some poems of your own. Use words about snakes. Write the words in snake shapes.

Rattlesnake Anagrams

Anagrams is a game where scrambled letters are rearranged to form words. A six-letter word related to rattlesnakes can be made out of each set of letters on the right. If you can't figure out the six letter rattlesnake word, look for a shorter word. For example, the word *tale* can easily be seen in the first set of letters. To figure out your score, give yourself 2 points for each letter you used. For each word in which you used all six letters, give yourself 20 extra points.

1. | T | T | A | L | E | R |
2. | S | E | A | S | L | C |
3. | C | E | S | S | T | U |
4. | E | I | K | R | S | T |
5. | E | I | P | R | S | V |
6. | A | E | K | N | S | S |
7. | I | O | P | O | N | S |
8. | A | D | G | N | L | S |

Answers

1. rattle   2. scales   3. scutes   4. strike   5. vipers   6. snakes   7. poison   8. glands

How many rattlesnakes can you find in this picture?

Make a Coiled Snake Pot

You will need: clay and toothpicks. (If you use salt clay, moisten the coils with water to make them stick together.)

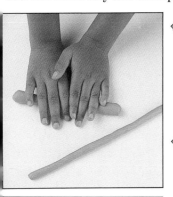

1 You will make the pot from the bottom up. Flatten a ball of clay by pressing it with your palm. The bottom needs to be as thick as your thumb and 3 to 4 inches across (8-10 centimeters).

2 Next, make a 13-inch (32.5-centimeter) coil by rolling clay back and forth between your hands and your work surface. Roll from the center of the coil to its ends to make the coil as thick as your finger.

3 Then put the clay coil around the edge of the flat bottom. Gently press the coil and the bottom together with your fingers. Also press together the two ends of the coil.

4 Make another 13-inch (32.5-centimeter) coil. Put the new coil on top of the one already in place. Gently press the two coils together. Then press together the two ends of the new coil.

5 Repeat Step 4 three more times. However, make the last coil 18 inches long (45 centimeters). Put this extra-long coil in place. Form a rattlesnake head out of the extra clay at one end.

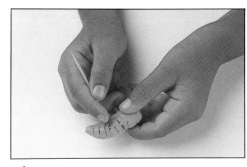

6 Form a rattle for the end of your snake's tail. Use a toothpick to add details to the rattle. Then, place the rattle on the top coil of the pot, opposite the head. Gently press the rattle to make it stick to the pot.

Salt Clay Recipe

3 cups flour (.75 liters)
1 cup salt (.25 liters)
½ cup vegetable oil (.125 liters)
1 cup water (.25 liters)

Thoroughly mix all ingredients by squeezing them with your hands until mixture sticks together. Store in a plastic bag to avoid drying.

Rattlesnake Word Puzzle

How many words can you make from the letters in the word RATTLESNAKE? You can use each letter only once in each word, except the letters **A**, **T**, and **E**. (These three letters can be used twice because there are two of them in the word *rattlesnake*.) Names of people and places don't count. Challenge your friends to see which of you can come up with the most words. Check your answers in a dictionary.

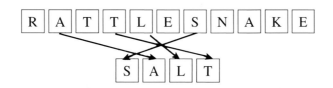

R A T T L E S N A K E

S A L T

Read More About Snakes

Rattlesnakes by Sherie Bargar and Linda Johnson. Vero Beach, Florida: Rourke Corp., 1988.

See eye-to-eye with snakes in this beautifully photographed book about rattlers. Learn more about how rattlesnakes look and act and where they live. Great for the rattlesnake lover and the report writer.

Rattlesnakes by G. Earl Chace. New York: Dodd, Mead, and Co., 1984.

Watch a young rattlesnake as she grows into an adult. Follow her as she lives on her own. Letting her instincts guide her, she finds food, escapes enemies, and eventually gives birth to young ones of her own.

Index